is for Eucharist
A Catholic Alphabet Book

written by
Michael Shoulders

illustrated by
Rick Anderson

Special thanks to:

Father Eric Fowlkes (Our Lady of the Lake Catholic Church, Hendersonville, TN)

Father David Gaffny (Immaculate Conception Church, Clarksville, TN)

Father Jean Baptise (Good Shepherd Parish, Decherd, TN)

Deacon Tim Winters (Immaculate Conception Church, Clarksville, TN)

Deacon Ken Long (All Saints Catholic Church, Knoxville, TN)

Terry Bradley (Teacher, Saint Francis of Asissi, Cordova, TN)

Kaylee Price, Eric Anderson, Laura and Courtland Foley

Father David O'Connor (St. Mary Basilica, Natchez, MS)

Anne McDaniel, photographer and friend Linda Martin

David, Transito, and Noah James

Father Mike O'Brien (Saint Richard Catholic Church, Jackson, MS)

Text Copyright ©2010 Michael Shoulders

Illustrations Copyright ©2010 Rick Anderson

Graphic Designer: Chuck Galey

Mockingbird Books
2023 Mossy Oak Circle
Clarksville, TN 37043

© Mockingbird Books

Library of Congress Control Number: 2010921855

10 9 8 7 6 5 4 3 2 1

Altar kisses begin the Mass.
Respect is shown here by the priest.
The host and blood are transformed here
For every Mass and special feasts.

At the start of Mass, the priest, concelebrants and deacons approach and kiss the altar. Since the altar represents Christ, this is a way of greeting and honoring Him. The first altar was the table on which Jesus and the Twelve Disciples celebrated the Last Supper. Pope St. Sixtus II (AD 257–258) decided every Mass should be celebrated on an altar. Since wood decays and some metals corrode, the Council of Epeaune (AD 517) decided altars must be consecrated of stone. Since then, altars have traditionally been made of stone. This is fitting since St. Paul said, "...and the rock was Christ." Altars often contain a small depository of the relics of a saint.

Journeys start with just one step.
So, where does a Catholic's begin?
To be Baptized is our first act.
Water washes away our sins.

Catholics see baptism as the beginning of their religious journey. "Living waters," or water that flows, "wash away" all sins from the person being baptized. Although some baptisms are done by immersion, some pour water over the head. Many baptisms are of infants but can be performed at any age. The Nicene Creed (AD 381) stated, "We believe in one baptism for the forgiveness of sins." When a priest baptizes he says, "[Name], I baptize you in the name of the Father, and of the Son, and of the Holy Spirit."

A symbol of the Catholic faith
Is the often-seen Crucifix.
It reminds us how Jesus died
By the sacrifice it depicts.

The crucifix is the principal symbol of the Christian religion. "Crucifix" is Latin (*cruci fixus*) meaning "one fixed to a cross" and represents Jesus's sacrifice. Prior to the 5th century, the Lamb of God represented Christ. The Council of Constantinople (AD 692) ordered, "Instead of the lamb, our Lord Jesus Christ will be shown hereafter in His human form in images so that we shall be led to remember His mortal life, His passion, and His death, which paid the ransom for mankind." The procession into the church is lead by a crucifix because Catholics "follow Christ." INRI stands for *Iesus Nazaraenus Rex Iudaeorum*, Latin for Jesus of Nazareth, King of the Jews.

John the Baptist baptized Jesus
In the waters of the Jordon.
God sent down His Holy Spirit
(The form of a Dove) to His Son.

The dove has long been used as a symbol for the Catholic faith, especially the Holy Spirit. The Bible mentions doves many times. In the Old Testament, Noah released a dove to search for land. When it returned with an olive branch, this showed the waters had receded. Ever since, the dove has symbolized deliverance and God's forgiveness. In the New Testament, St. Luke wrote, "And Jesus being baptized, forthwith came out of the water: and lo, the heavens were opened to Him: and He saw the Spirit of God descending as a dove, and coming upon Him." The dove represents peace, especially when depicted with an olive branch.

At every mass the priest offers
The sacrament of Eucharist.
Catholics believe through host and blood
That Christ is present in our midst.

Eucharist, also called Holy Communion, describes the celebration of the Mass. It is a symbol of divine grace for the believer. As the priest speaks words of consecration our Lord transforms the bread and wine into the body and blood of Christ. Catholics classify the Eucharist as a sacrament when God is uniquely present, an outward sign of inward grace. The Eucharist is the sacramental celebration of the Paschal Mystery: Christ dying, passing from Earth, and ascending to a life with the Father. Catholics may receive communion at every Mass; however, they must receive it at least once a year. Eucharist means "thanksgiving."

Faith is believing something's true
And this belief is not in vain.
Faith is trusting in God's grace and
His Son's resurrection's our gain.

Faith is from the Latin word *fidem*, meaning trust and a belief in future outcomes. We have faith a chair will hold us and we show our belief each time we sit. However, faith is not a single act, but an entire way of life and leads to an active life of obedience to God, the one being trusted. Faith is the agreement of the mind with truths revealed by God. Faith, means, then, "I believe you."

Gospels: Matthew, Mark, Luke, and John
Are four ways the "Good News" is spread.
From Jesus's Bethlehem birth
To resurrection from the dead.

Gospels are writings describing the life of Jesus. The term "Gospels" usually refers to the first four books of the New Testament: Matthew, Mark, Luke, and John. The Gospels were probably written in the years from AD 65 to 100. Many scholars believe Mark's Gospel was written first. The first three Gospels, Mark, Matthew, and Luke, have similar incidents and teachings and are called "synoptic," meaning common views. They include Jesus's birth, the Sermon on the Mount, the Beatitudes, and the Last Supper. John's Gospel mentions many miracles. The Gospels are read aloud during Mass.

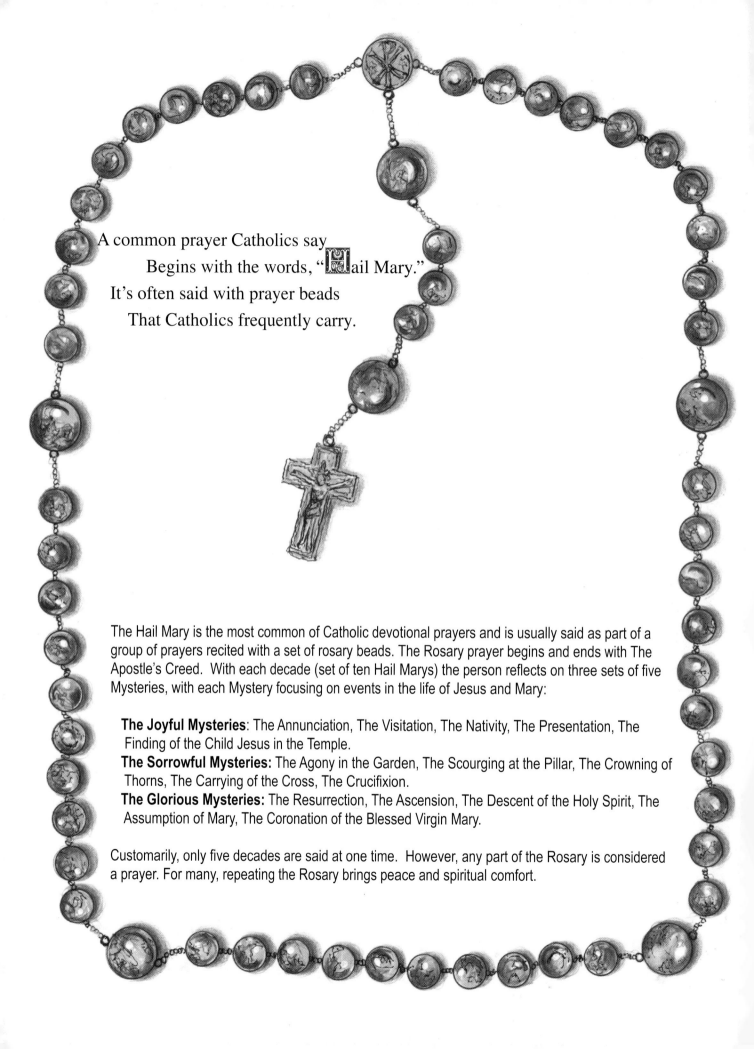

A common prayer Catholics say
Begins with the words, "Hail Mary."
It's often said with prayer beads
That Catholics frequently carry.

The Hail Mary is the most common of Catholic devotional prayers and is usually said as part of a group of prayers recited with a set of rosary beads. The Rosary prayer begins and ends with The Apostle's Creed. With each decade (set of ten Hail Marys) the person reflects on three sets of five Mysteries, with each Mystery focusing on events in the life of Jesus and Mary:

The Joyful Mysteries: The Annunciation, The Visitation, The Nativity, The Presentation, The Finding of the Child Jesus in the Temple.
The Sorrowful Mysteries: The Agony in the Garden, The Scourging at the Pillar, The Crowning of Thorns, The Carrying of the Cross, The Crucifixion.
The Glorious Mysteries: The Resurrection, The Ascension, The Descent of the Holy Spirit, The Assumption of Mary, The Coronation of the Blessed Virgin Mary.

Customarily, only five decades are said at one time. However, any part of the Rosary is considered a prayer. For many, repeating the Rosary brings peace and spiritual comfort.

Sometimes, during a part of Mass
The priest or a deacon may swing
A thurible burning Incense
To honor holy, sacred things.

Thuribles hold hot coals on which incense is burned. The smoke symbolizes prayers rising to heaven and purifying all it touches. The clergy use incense to bless the altar, the Gospel, priests, bread and wine, and even the congregation.

Thurible swinging:
- Three sets of three swings: the Blessed Sacrament, the gifts at the altar, the celebrant, and people.
- Three sets of two swings: images, relics, and other sacramentals.

Jesus was born in Bethlehem,
The Father's one and only son.
He came to tell us God loves us
And He is there for every one.

Born in Bethlehem, Jesus was the son of Mary. By the time He was 12, Jesus impressed scholars in Jerusalem's temples with His understanding of religious laws. Nothing is known about His life between the ages of 12 and 30. He began preaching at the age of 30 and continued until His death at 33. Many people witnessed Jesus performing miracles such as turning water into wine or making the blind see. Jesus talked about the evils of injustice and spoke about how much God loves us. Jesus created a connection between God and Earth's people.

Kneeling shows our humility
When we pray and when we reflect.
As Catholics begin a prayer
We bow our heads or genuflect.

Kneeling shows humility, submission, and reverence. Luke tells us (22:40–41) that Jesus knelt to pray, "And when He came to the place, He said to them: Pray, lest ye enter into temptation. And He was withdrawn away from them a stone's cast. And kneeling down, He prayed." Catholics also genuflect (bend one knee to the ground) to indicate a submission of heart and mind to the Presence of Christ. Catholics genuflect or bow upon entering a pew at church to signify knowledge that Christ is present in the tabernacle.

The day before Christ died, He shared a Last Supper with His Twelve Apostles. It is generally agreed the meal was held on a Thursday, in the upper room of a house just outside Jerusalem. The Last Supper is believed to have been held on the 14th or 15th of Nisan, the Jewish month near the current months of March or April. On that night, Jesus took bread, gave thanks, broke the bread and said, "This is my body, which is for you; do this in remembrance of me."

At the **L**ast Supper, Jesus and
His chosen Twelve sat down to dine.
"This is my body. This is my
Blood," He said of the bread and wine.

In the same way, after supper, He took the cup, saying, "This cup is the new covenant in my blood; do this, whenever you drink it, in remembrance of me." Jesus also gave a sermon called "farewell discourse." Jesus said He would suffer after the meal. Jesus revealed that one of His Apostles would betray Him and one would deny Him three times. The Last Supper is seen as the "First Eucharist."

The Third Commandment reminds us:
Keep the Sabbath a Holy Day.
Attending Mass allows us to
Sing, listen, tithe, reflect, and pray.

Jesus instituted the Mass at His Last Supper. Since Mass repeats the Last Supper, the celebrants participate in the life of Christ. Mass strengthens a bond with Jesus. During Mass, the priest acts in the person of Christ and we celebrate the memory of the Lord.

During Mass, Catholics stand for prayers and the proclamation of the Gospel. Catholics sit during readings and homilies as they are instructional in nature. Catholics kneel in adoration for the consecration of bread and wine and before and after receiving Holy Communion. The celebrant must be in a state of grace with fasting at least one hour prior to receiving the Eucharist.

The text of the Mass varies depending on the day, but follows this basic order:

I. Introductory Rites
      Entrance Procession
      Greeting
      Penitential Rite
      Kyrie
      Gloria
      Opening Prayer

II. Liturgy of the Word
      Bible Readings
      Responsorial Psalm
      Gospel Reading
      Homily or Sermon
      Profession of Faith
        (Nicene or Apostle's Creed)
      Prayers

III. Liturgy of the Eucharist
      Presentation of Gifts
      Prayer Over the Offerings
      Consecrating

IV. Communion Rite
      Lord's Prayer
      Sign of Peace
      Breaking of the Bread
      Holy Communion

V. Concluding Rite
      Announcements
      Blessing
      Dismissal

Nativity is often used
As a word for Jesus's birth.
The son of the Virgin Mary,
He is The Savior born on Earth.

The Nativity is celebrated on December 25. For Catholics, this time is second in importance only to Easter. The Gospels of Matthew and Luke describe the story of the nativity.

Mary learned from the angel Gabriel that she would bear a child. Gabriel said the Holy Spirit would "come upon her" and Jesus would be a Virgin birth. Mary and Joseph traveled from Nazareth to Bethlehem, Joseph's ancestral home, to register for the census. Finding no rooms available in the inn, Mary gave birth to Jesus in a feeding trough. An angel announced the good news to shepherds in nearby fields.

Adam was tempted and he ate
Fruit from the one forbidden tree.
When Adam disobeyed the Lord
Original Sin came to be.

The first or "original sin" was Adam's disobedience of God. Original sin is the lack of holiness humans are born into, not actual sins they have committed. Adam's descendents are born in a state of sinfulness. Baptism washes away this original sin. Some falsely believe "Immaculate Conception" means Mary gave birth to Jesus without a human father. Instead, it means Mary was born without the stain of original sin.

A Penance is a sacrament
Where a confessor states their sins.
With sorrow they plead forgiveness
And try not to do it again.

Penance is sometimes called the Sacrament of Reconciliation. Catholics begin by saying, "Bless me Father, for I have sinned." The person reveals their sins to the priest. The priest may ask questions to clarify the motives behind the sin. The priest asks if the person is sorry and tells the person to say the Act of Contrition. The priest assigns a penance and says, "Your sins are forgiven. Go and sin no more." To be reconciled to God, the penitent performs the penance to show sorrow for the sin committed. The most common penance is saying prayers such as the Hail Mary or Lord's Prayer. The priest has a "sacramental seal" meaning he must keep secret what he hears in confession.

Quadragesima is a time
Of reflection and giving praise.
This time begins on Ash Wednesday
And spans across Lent's forty days.

Quadragesima (/kwä′drə jā′zi mə/) is any forty-day period to imitate Christ's example by fasting, praying and abstaining from festivities. The most common quadragesima is Lent and counts the weekdays from Ash Wednesday to Easter Sunday. On Ash Wednesday, the faithful have ashes placed on the forehead as a sign of repentance. There are other references to forty days in the Bible: Moses's forty days on Mount Sinai; Elijah's forty days walking to Mount Horeb; God made it rain for forty days; and Jesus fasted for forty days and was tempted by the devil in the desert of Judea.

The capital of Italy
Is the ancient city of Rome.
Also called "The City of Popes"
It's where the Pontiff makes his home.

The smallest country in the world is situated totally within the city limits of Rome, Italy. Vatican City is a 110-acre city-state with the Holy Father being the head-of-state. Because Vatican City is home to the Holy Father, Rome is known as "The City of Popes." The most prominent building in Vatican City is St. Peter's Basilica.

In 42 AD St. Peter left Jerusalem and traveled to Rome. At that time, Nero ruled the Roman Empire and persecuted millions of Christians. Between 64 and 67 AD, Nero ordered St. Peter's death. Feeling unworthy to die as Jesus died, St. Peter chose to be crucified upside down. St. Peter is considered the first Pope of the Catholic Church. Two hundred years later, Emperor Constantine made Christianity the religion of the State and built a basilica where, some say, the tomb of St. Peter is located. After it fell into disrepair, a new basilica was begun in 1506 AD. It holds 60,000 people.

Seven Sacraments are offered
For every Catholic to embrace.
        A sacrament is often called
                An outward sign of inward grace.

Sacraments have been defined as outward signs of inward grace, instituted by Christ for our sanctification. A sign means it stands for something else. A red light, for instance, means stop. In baptism, water illustrates the "washing away" of sin.

During a sacrament, three things are present:
  • words are said
  • promises are made
  • a mark or symbol is used.
The seven holy sacraments are: Baptism, Eucharist, Reconciliation, Confirmation, Marriage, Holy Orders, and the Anointing of the Sick.

Hosts not consumed during the Mass
Are stored in a reverent place.
Tabernacles reserve the hosts
In a prominent, holy case.

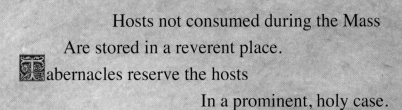

Tabernacles are locked and immovable containers in which the Eucharist is stored. In early Christianity, celebrants took consecrated hosts home and stored them for those unable to attend the Mass. Later, the Church established a practice of keeping the Eucharist in vessels only in churches. A sanctuary lamp, often red or white and placed near the tabernacle, indicates and honors Christ's presence in the tabernacle. Often, the tabernacle is veiled with colors similar to the priest's vestments. Catholics may bow or genuflect toward the tabernacle as a sign of respect and adoration.

Holy oils are used for Unction.
They're blessed by Bishops once a year.
The jars are kept in an ambry.
Unction means to anoint or smear.

On Holy Thursday, at a Chrism Mass, bishops bless anointing Oils of the Sick (used for the ill), Oils of the Catechumens (used for adults joining the church), and Sacred Chrism (used for baptism, confirmation, and Holy Orders). Priests carry the oils to each parish where they are stored in an ambry. The word ambry is from the Latin *armarium*, meaning cupboard, closet, or chest. The previous year's oils are burned. Holy Oils are also used for consecrating bells, chalices, church walls, and altars.

estments can be several colors:

        Red, green, purple, golden or white.

The colors vary, day to day,

    Depending on the Mass and rite.

Vestments are garments worn by the clergy. The chasuble, a sleeveless outer garment, is worn over a white alb. The alb is held in place at the waist by a long cord called a cincture. The stole is a long scarf worn around the neck by the priest and over the shoulder by the deacon.

White = Christmas and Easter seasons, celebrations of Mary, masses for the dead, Saints' Days.

Red = Palm Sunday, Good Friday, Pentecost Sunday, and feast days of Martyrs

Green = Ordinary Times

Violet = Lent and Advent

Rose = 3rd Sunday of Advent and 4th Sunday of Lent

Golden = substituted for White, Red, or Green

Holy Water is often found
In holy fonts on church wall shelves.
It reminds us of baptisms
When we use it to bless ourselves.

Water symbolizes cleansing and purity. From Genesis to Revelation, water is mentioned hundreds of times in the Bible. Jesus walked on water, turned it into wine, and used it to wash His disciples' feet. Perhaps water's most important use is in baptism. Crossing ourselves with water from holy water fonts when we enter and leave church reminds us of our own baptism. The Bible reminds us that without water there is no life, and without Christ, there is no eternal life.

When communion is not received
An  is formed across the chest.
The person does not take the host
Instead, the faithful will be blessed.

Those who are baptized, are in full communion with the Catholic Church, have received their first Holy Communion, and are in the state of grace, may receive Holy Communion. In some places, others may participate in the Eucharist by folding their arms across their chests in the form of an "X" when approaching the altar. This lets the server know the participant wishes to receive a blessing. The priest will place his hands gently on the head and ask for God's blessing.

Liturgical Years encompass:

Ordinary time and Lent,

Easter Triduum, Easter Season,

Pentecost, Christmas, and Advent.

Liturgical years include the celebrations that take place during one church year. Different aspects of Jesus's life are told during a Liturgical year. The Liturgical year begins with Advent. The cycle includes Christmas, Ordinary Time, Lent, and Easter Time.

There are three sets of readings assigned for Sundays and special days. In Year A, the Gospel of Matthew is read; in Year B, the Gospel of Mark; in Year C, the Gospel of Luke. The Gospel of John focuses on the risen life of Christ and is predominately read during Lent, Easter, Advent and Christmas.

Once upon a long time ago,
A clergy's shaved head was the norm.
Churches were often cold and damp.
A Zucchetto kept bare heads warm.

Tonsure is the ancient practice in some churches of shaving the tops of the heads of the ecclesiastic. It symbolized the rejection of worldly fashions. Since churches were often cold, the clergy wore a zucchetto (/Zu*chet"to/), an eight-panel cap with a stem. A zucca is Italian for "small gourd." Because its appearance is similar to a small pumpkin, the cap is called zucchetto. Zucchetti (plural) can be found in paintings over seven hundred years old. The Holy Father wears a white zucchetto; cardinals wear red; bishops wear purple; priests wear black.

The Our Father
Our Father, who art in heaven, hallowed be thy name. Thy kingdom come; thy will be done on Earth as it is in heaven. Give us this day our daily bread; and forgive us our trespasses as we forgive those who trespass against us; and lead us not into temptation, but deliver us from evil. Amen.

The Hail Mary
Hail Mary full of grace, the Lord is with thee. Blessed art thou among women, and blessed is the fruit of thy womb, Jesus. Holy Mary, mother of God, pray for us sinners now and at the hour of our death. Amen.

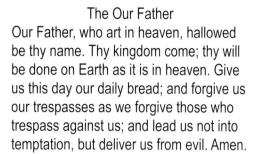

The Hail Holy Queen
Hail! Holy Queen, mother of mercy, our life, our sweetness, and our hope. To you we cry, poor banished children of Eve. To you do we send up our sighs, mourning and weeping in this valley of tears. Turn then, O most gracious advocate, your eyes of mercy toward us, and after this our exile, show unto us the blessed fruit of your womb, Jesus. O clement! O loving! O sweet Virgin Mary! Pray for us, O holy mother of God, that we may be made worthy of the promises of Christ. Amen.

The Glory Be
Glory Be to the Father, and to the Son, and to the Holy Spirit. As it was in the beginning, is now and ever shall be, world without end. Amen.

The Apostle's Creed
I believe in God, the Father almighty, Creator of heaven and earth. And in Jesus Christ, His only son, our Lord; who was conceived by the Holy Spirit, born of the Virgin Mary, suffered under Pontius Pilate, was crucified, died, and was buried. He descended into hell; the third day He rose again from the dead; He ascended into heaven, sits at the right hand of God, the Father almighty. From thence He shall come to judge the living and the dead. I believe in the Holy spirit, the holy Catholic Church, the communion of saints, the forgiveness of sins, the resurrection of the body, and life everlasting. Amen.